Dream, Girl

A Collection of Poetry & Prose

Julia Yee

DREAM, GIRL

Praise for *Dream, Girl*

"Each poem within this collection felt like a mantra, an affirmation of confidence. Each piece is a reminder that we must never stop dreaming, never stop believing in ourselves, and if we do, to remember and come back to all that we are. This is a lovely collection to remind you to never stop sharing your creativity, or the wonder one holds for the world."
— Tiffiny Rose Allen, Author of *At The Beginning Of Yesterday*

"*Dream, Girl* is a wonderful collection of poetry that feels deeply connected to the roots of being a woman. We are powerful and gentle beings who can exist simply in all the right ways if we believe it. Julia Yee makes you believe it with her lovely words, on each page."
— Kendall Hope, Author of *The Willow Weepings*

"In *Dream, Girl,* Julia Yee holds readers' hands like an older sister giving you a deep talk on a warm summer night. Through her own revelations, she shares both personal experience and universal guidance. Her writing meanders between thoughtful prose and flowing verse to create a text simultaneously instructive and insightful. *Dream, Girl* lives up to its title. Readers will find softness in examples of Yee's dreaming and be reminded of how to dream themselves."
— Kira Rosemarie, Author of *Moon/Season*

"*Dream, Girl* is the quintessential motivational poetry book for any woman who needs to be encouraged to keep going after her dreams and believing in herself. Each page, was empowering and made me feel seen, heard and inspired not to give up on my goals."
— Annie Vazquez, Author of *My Little Prayer Book: 75 Prayers, Poems and Mantras for Illumination*

"A beautiful debut, *Dream, Girl* is courage, inspiration and strength in a lovely, lively and colorful collection that you'll want to take with you everywhere you go. Each poem is one step closer to believing in your creativity, believing in your dreams and believing in yourself. This book is for every dreamer that needs a reminder to dream."
— Flor Ana, Author of *The Truth About Love*

Edited by Flor Ana Mireles

1st Edition | 01

Hardback ISBN: 979-8-9880379-6-5

Paperback ISBN: 979-8-9880379-5-8

First Published August 2023

For inquiries and bulk orders, please email:
indieearthpublishinghouse@gmail.com

Printed in the United States

1 2 3 4 5 6 7 8 9

Indie Earth Publishing Inc.
| Miami, FL |

Dream, Girl

This book is for Her.
You know Her,
your Dream Girl.
The one you are growing
and healing
and loving
and forever becoming.
And to do so, you have to dream, girl.

Be both the dreamer and the dream.

Dream, Girl

Do you remember Her?
The one you search for?
There is a forgotten world inside you,
so much more beautiful and powerful than the one around you.
Long ago, in your ancient history,
the floods came and they took your knowing away,
drowning your palaces of light and temples of your own worship.

You built yourself a ship and braved the storm;
when once more you found solid ground,
you built a world so shiny and new
that you almost forgot about the one you left behind.
Will you find your way back home?
Or will She be forever sunken in the depths of your safe unknowing?
A lost world, reduced to myth,
like so many others before Her.

It's easy to forget who you really are in this world. And it's ok if you do, for who among us hasn't? Getting lost is a part of life, and finding your way back home is the journey of a lifetime.

We are more than we are taught to believe. We are more than the things we have been told and the things we have told ourselves. We have all fought so hard to get to where we are now; the strength that it took to get this far is beautiful. But if you have ever wondered if there is even more depth to this life and to your soul, know that you can find it, and that you can find Her. You can find the love, the peace, and the joy that you are searching for. You can find the person you have always been, who is deserving of all those things and more.

The first step is simply believing that you are worthy of being found.

Dream, Girl

I asked to be seen.
And yet, I did not dare show myself,
scared to be too much,
but at the same time, not enough.
I yearned to be heard.
And yet, I remained too afraid to speak,
my desires trapped on the tip of my tongue.
I sought acceptance at every turn,
in every smile or frown.
And in doing so, I deprived myself of my own acceptance,
the only one I need.

It's normal to want to be seen, heard, and accepted by others. More than that, you deserve to be. But most of all, you deserve your own acceptance. Self-acceptance is not a linear journey, nor does it come all at once. It is a path, and it will lead you back to yourself.

So many of us are shamed
for not knowing our worth.
You are worth so much more,
they say.
You deserve better,
they say.
And though they may be right,
the reality is that it is the journey of a lifetime
to know our worth.
From people to purpose, to love and life,
we determine our worth a thousand different ways every day,
and it takes a thousand small steps
to become all that we could be.

It's ok if you're not there yet—wherever it is you want to be. It's ok if you never get there. What is more important, is that you are moving. Backwards, forwards, in circles—it doesn't matter. Because as long as you are moving, you will get to where you need to be, whether you want to or not, and despite what those around you might say. The discovery of who we really are is such a personal journey. The things we learn, and the way we learn them in this lifetime are beyond comparison. So do the thing, make the mistake, learn again and again, and know you're not the only one. Although it might look different for each and every one of us, we are all simply figuring it out the only way we can.

Dream, Girl

Every night, I beg for a world that is gentle and kind;
yet, every day, I tear myself apart.
It is no wonder then, if my outer world mirrors that coldness
that has crept inside,
and like the harshest of winters,
with wind that whips and burns everything it touches,
stripped me bare.
It seems like all I can do is wait
and trust that spring will come again.
Or maybe, I will take a step inside myself and
tumble through my tangled desires,
summit my highest fears,
reach through the clouds,
grapple the sun,
and pull my light back to me,
to let my scorched earth bloom again.
Or perhaps, it will take a mixture
of trusting the natural cycle of seasons
and the continuous resolve to face my depths and heights,
if not unflinchingly,
then with understanding and hope.

When I think that life is being cruel to me/I sit back and realize/that life is simply happening/and it is I who is being cruel to myself

We beat ourselves up in so many ways every single day. Even when you want to stop, the cycle can feel unbreakable and unstoppable. So, take a breath. Stop beating yourself up over beating yourself up. Get to know yourself even deeper. Ask why and why and why you feel this way. And when you've exhausted all the questions and answers and you still feel trapped inside yourself, open a door within, get out, and discover that rugged inner landscape of yours. Run your hands along your scars. Climb the dizzying heights of your desires. Get lost in your wild hopes and unnamed fears. When asking questions isn't enough, let yourself feel into every part of you. Traverse the landscape of your soul, even if there is no sun to guide you. Open yourself to the darkness when it comes, but know that warmth and light will return again, and you will bloom over and over. And when that happens, go and explore that part of you, too.

I search my heart
for the intensity of feelings that have plagued it for so long.
The heartache, the restlessness, the desperation
I thought had become a part of me as I gave up
on the healing nature of time because time seemed to only yield
more absence, longing, and questions.
But today, I search my heart,
prodding its pain points, bracing myself, and
for the first time in a long time,
I feel peace,
a fullness where there was once a gaping hole,
and I am flooded with relief.
For there is a delicious quality to inner calm
as it settles smoothly within you,
flowing like sweet syrup—
a balm over your scars.
It is the feeling of your power
coming back to you.

When all you've known for so long is fear and stress and heartache, these big, dark emotions can feel like they are meant to stay. Feel them and learn from them while they are here, and then, let yourself be lured back to your calm. With time, let your own calming presence, like a balm made from your own moon and stars, heal you. Draw from your own power and let peace back into your life.

Dream, Girl

My heart spins in circles.
She is dizzy and doesn't know which way to turn.
She feels everything too deeply.
She cries hard and laughs harder.
She relishes the pain, but longs for comfort.
She is burnt, she is weary,
but she also has chaotic spurts of energy.
She is everywhere, but she just wants to be somewhere
with a specific someone.
Oh, my heart,
she knows not, but her unknowing has an innocent beauty to it,
a purity of hope that carries her on.
Oh, my heart,
I hope one day she will find a place
to rest and catch her breath,
sweaty and smiling.
And when she is ready,
she will look up and she will know,
with all her knowing,
where she is,
and where she is going.

At times, my heart seems so very far away from me, like she is a different entity entirely. One who has more love to give that I could ever conceive. One who is stronger than I give her credit for being. One who feels more deeply than even I do. I want to help her, to save her, but I don't always feel equipped to do so. She moves so fast. She tries so hard. I can only observe her from afar, worried that any movement of mine will scare her away. But I am moving closer and closer. Perhaps one day, she will look up and recognize me as the one she has been looking for all along.

Dream, Girl

When all of me feels like drifting away,
pulled towards hazy shorelines
by wayward winds and blinding storms,
I drop anchor in my heart of hearts,
mooring myself in my own depths,
the parts of me that will not be shaken,
pushed around by ripping currents,
or lured away by siren calls;
the part of me that knows how to hold on,
be still and stand strong.

When you feel like you are losing yourself or that life is overwhelming you, and that you have nowhere left to run, or hide, there will always be one place where you can feel safe. A place where you will be welcomed and taken care of—readied again for what will come next. And that place is the part of you that is the most you. That piece of you that can never be shaken or broken. That piece of you that has taken the blows and has come out stronger and more sure. Sink into that part of you. Bathe in your own light. Let yourself remember who you really are.

Get lost in the now around you—
in the sparkles dancing in the wake of a boat,
in the way light is falling through the trees,
in the way the people around you are going about their lives,
in the very feel of their air,
as it trickles down your throat
and inflates your lungs.

You don't need to search and strive for a beautiful life. It is your birthright, and it is all around you all of the time, if only you look. Sometimes, it takes getting lost in the now around you to find everything you were looking for. For, oftentimes, the way is there, in those in-between moments where you think nothing is happening, but in reality, it is the very essence of life that is passing you by. Find that essence. Let it ground you, reinvigorate you, and revive you.

In a society bent on distilling our humanness,
and understanding what we are,
and constantly asking,
why,
why,
why,
sometimes, I just want to be a thing.
A beautiful thing.

In a world obsessed with moving on, moving forward, and moving fast,
faster and faster,
I just want to be still.
A still
beautiful
thing.

Sometimes, we can't help but ask why. Why are we here? Why has this happened, or why hasn't it happened yet? Sometimes, we can't help but want to throw ourselves to the wind and let it whisk us away to the future we have been wishing for, letting our present bend and blur around us, in hope of something better coming.

But sometimes, it is best to forget the questions, the wondering, the waiting, the rushing. Sometimes, the answer is to just let yourself be. Wrap your mind in as much stillness as you can muster and let your body melt into the air that surrounds it. Let your still, beautiful being represent a rebellion against a world that tells you to be everything but.

Dream, Girl

I don't want to be soft, rolling flesh.
I want to be iron,
perfectly welded.
Or carved from stone,
every line and curve immaculately chiseled,
cleanly contained,
unblemished, elegant, and cold.
But I am warm, heated, and undone,
unraveling at the seams
and blurred around the edges.

Be soft. Be uncontained and untamed. Be warm, feeling, and imperfect. Be more than what you are told to be. Be undefined and unrefined by the laws of men—a work of art entirely of your own creation.

Enough of
squeezing into things.
Enough of
ripping space into the fabric of the world
with nails and teeth.
Enough of
feeling too big and too small at the same time
in all the wrong places.
Enough.

I want to create a life that fits me.
A way of thinking that becomes me.
A sense of being that finally feels like She has made it home.

From such a young age, we are told we are too big and too small. That we need to be bigger and smaller in so many different ways. Our bodies, our voices, our dreams.

For so long, we have been told we need to fit into things. Like tight dresses, skinny jeans, and strappy heels. We are told we need to conform to the world around us so we may hopefully find our place in it.

And when we don't fit, we are told to try harder. To sweat and starve and burn ourselves out. Because surely after all that effort, we will have finally carved out a space for ourselves.

We deserve better than that. We deserve a world and a life that fits us as we are.

Let yourself expand, expand, and expand, taking up as much space as you want, and afterwards, let the world settle around YOU.

Dream, Girl

I used to think there was a monster inside of me,
something that was fury-born
that yearned to rage and roar.
Only later did I come to learn
She was not a monster,
but simply a wild little girl.
One who longed to shriek with laughter
and howl with delight,
who had too many feelings inside of Her
that She felt like She had to hide.

Let yourself be flooded with emotion. Laugh too loud and cry too hard. Let the wild inside of you be free. Even when it seems like you can't feel anything at all, feel that nothingness as wholly as you can, for your feelings can never be taken away from you.

Search for the things that light you up and set off a spark in your heart—you will never be lead astray. And throughout your search, if you ever stop and wonder what you're doing and why, know that you're doing it for Her, your inner child. Your you-est you. Let Her experience the world in all its ecstatic glory, and before you know it, you won't just be surviving, you'll be thriving.

My heart is not one of stone or steel,
protective and unyielding against the blows.
Nor is it one of glass, so hard and so fragile—
too easily shattered.
No, my heart is something soft,
like a pincushion,
into which the sharpest spears are welcomed home
and gently held.
Too loving, too open, too kind,
and yet, unbreakable.

Let yourself be soft and giving and kind. Because what they don't tell you, is that you can be soft and giving and kind and also so incredibly strong. To love deeply, give openly, and receive freely, is to live fiercely.

And when that beautiful unrelenting love in your heart is tortured and trampled and shot through with darts, when your heart feels irreparably broken, fear not. For it is the softest of hearts that can hold space for the sharpest pains. And though it might seem like an unbearable burden, know that slowly, so slowly, that pain is being churned into even more love by your big, unbreakably soft heart.

Dream, Girl

She was painfully pretty;
a ferocious beauty,
like heaven and hell together
in one earthly body,
decadent, resplendent, and lost.
In other words,
She was a woman.

Being a woman is beautiful. Being a woman is painful. Being a woman is dangerous.

We are persecuted relentlessly, for so many differing and opposing reasons, across the globe, and throughout history. And still, we have survived, persevered, thrived. Because, more than anything, we are dangerously powerful. For we contain within us multitudes that cannot be limited to time, space, or even the heavens alone.

So, unleash everything that is holding you back. Get lost within yourself, your power, your world of infinite possibility. Get lost pursuing yourself. Get lost in exploration of your own love and peace. Show the world what it is to be a woman.

Dream, Girl

I have always felt too young
during any given period of my life.
Every day and every second I gaze at others,
wondering how they got there so elegantly and sure.
How they came to that moment
without flailing and grasping like I think I do.
And the more I move through life, the younger I feel.
For the world only grows vaguer and more confusing.
Or maybe it's just me who is vague and confused—
forever a little girl in a world of too many possibilities.

If you've ever wondered how everyone else seems so much more grown up than you, know you are not alone. And by grown up, I don't mean mature. No, being grown up is defined by something more vague and arbitrary than that. Like in the way, one day, laughter takes on a harsh, tinny timbre. A glassy finish, that doesn't ring out or last for long. In the way feelings are so proudly suppressed. In the way hearty excitement for things big and small is looked down upon. In the way elegance becomes synonymous with being silent, still, cold. In the way lives become shinier on the outside than they are on the inside.

Will there always be something too innocent and undone about the way you move through the world? Maybe. And maybe that's not a bad thing either.

When I was younger, I may have always wanted to be older, but I have never wanted to be a grown up.

Dream, Girl

I wish I could take my sticky sweet desires
that cling to me, like cotton slicked with sweat,
and fling them over the edge of the earth.
I can only imagine that the relief would be immense:
the weight of my wants gone,
if only for a moment.
And in that moment,
so light I would feel
I think I would float right up into the sky.
Perhaps then,
I would finally gain some perspective.

Oftentimes, it can feel like we are defined by the things we want in this life: our ability to get them, our success at having done so, or our failure to do so. So, it's almost funny to think that we are not, in fact, defined by such fickle ideals. Whether they are in regard to the material, or not. Even if that ideal is such a thing as love itself.

Wanting love does not make you sad, or weak, or less than. Losing love does not lessen your capacity to love and be loved. Not receiving the love that you desire does not reduce your worth as a person who is deserving of love. Nor does having that love make one more loveable or worthy of love than anyone else. You can replace the word love here with any other of your desires, and it would still be true.

Cast off the weight of your desires from your shoulders. Let them guide you, let them inspire you, but never let them define you.

Dream, Girl

Already, you turn your back,
ready to flee as fast as you have come,
only to break into me again later.
Don't go yet.
Sit with me awhile.
I want to get to know you.
Pain?
Shame?
Discomfort?
I won't label you,
or run, or hide from you.
Not this time.
No, I will be kind to you, and welcome you in,
letting you sink into me,
bore holes into my bones,
etch scars into my soft tissue, and
dissipate between my nerves.
Only then will I let you go,
knowing that when you return,
you will return as an old friend
who may take root,
curling smooth leaves and
fragrant flowers over old wounds.

Experiencing and expressing emotion are beautiful things, but they do not make us. Yet, they can help us discover who we are. What makes you light up with joy? What makes you curl up in fear? Instead of judging the emotions that pass through us, constantly jostling for our attention, stealing our breath, upsetting our stomach, and confusing our heart, sit with them. Even the ones that scare you.

There are parts of ourselves that we are not always willing to discover, and if we are willing, it's difficult to know where to begin. So let your emotions show you who you are underneath them.

I want to be struck dumb in the face of beauty
and spend a whole week happily dreaming.
I want to float like a leaf on water
and delight in the forgetfulness of not doing,
but *being.*

Let yourself be awestruck every single day of your existence. Be so mesmerized by your life, you forget about everything else but the current moment.

Let your mind loose in the infinity that surrounds you.
Let it dance.
Let it play.
Let it laugh.

Free your mind from the bounds it has grown accustomed to. Free your mind from the constraints you put on it, that society puts on it. Let your mind think and feel the most wonderful and wild things without restraint. From the deepest thoughts to the lightest day-dreams, let your mind go, and see what comes.

Dream, Girl

How could you have known?
When all you ever knew were stormy seas,
you thought this must be it—
my safe harbour.

You have braved the toughest waves,
made it through the harshest winds.
Though your hull was scratched and sails torn,
you thought you were fine,
that this was it for you.

You are, but it is not.

Listen to the voice that tells you
there is a harbour built just for you,
where you may rest your battered vessel.
Search for it,
even if it means leaving
your old world behind.

Imagine a peace
softer and more loving that what you are familiar with.
Hold that vision in your mind's eye,
and like a lighthouse on a dark night,
your dreams will guide you home.

If you have ever wished that there was more to life than what you now know, trust that there is. If you have ever wondered if you are worthy of more love than what you have let yourself believe you are limited to, know that you are. If you are wondering how to find that life and that love you are looking for, turn to your dreams, for that is where it all starts. Dream of a life that fills you with excitement. Dream of a love that fills your heart. Dream with purpose and untamed abandon. Those dreams will guide you to where you are meant to go.

Dream, Girl

I am tired of living my life through other people,
planning every word, thought, reaction
as a response to someone else.

I am tired of scrounging for what I can get
instead of what I deserve,
latching onto minuscule acts of kindness
and fleeting moments of intimacy.

I am tired and I need to wake up
to what life could be if I lived my life as if I owned it
instead of renting it by the hour,
borrowing stolen moments
that were too beautiful to bear
and so they vanished as quickly as they had come.

I am going to make myself a promise,
to sleep all night and dream all day
so I won't be so tired anymore.

It is easy to forget that your life belongs to you and you alone. The choices you can make are unlimited and untouchable by the judgements of others. The most beautiful moments in your life are not there by chance; they are meant for you to revel in and recognize so that you will come to know your happiness by heart and be able to call it in whenever you want. This life can be as big and bright as you can imagine, if only you let yourself do so. Imagine the sublime, the divine, the exceptional, and you will find that you are more awake than ever before.

The fragility of our world
can seem overwhelming in its delicacy.
How easy it is for things to change,
to end,
to break.
But then, I think of how much strength there is
in the fragile nature of our being.
How strong we must be to exist and persist,
flying on gossamer wings.

There is beauty in knowing everything can change—there is no hope without it. We either hope that things will change for the better, or we hope that they will never change at all. Life goes on in such cycles of hoping, and changing, and hoping once more. So, remember: you are never stuck, you are never hopeless, and just by being here, you are stronger than you think.

It feels like the very air around me is spun glass—
one wrong move
and the world, *my world,*
will come crashing down around me, and
the fragility of my carefully constructed life paralyses me.
But then, a small, knowing voice whispers,
let it fall apart.
Dare the tectonic plates that hold your world together
to crash into each other.
Let your past shift and crumble,
and see the soaring mountains that rise amidst the destruction.
Remember, when your world is poised to shatter,
the universe will be open to you anew.

Falling apart can be beautiful, too. Let it be beautiful, and get ready for what is always coming next. When your world feels like it is breaking apart or like it is already in ruins, raise your head and steady your heart. For when you look around you, *really look,* you might see the silver-bright edges of your forgotten dreams shimmering in front of you.

I've finally tired of running away.
So instead, I'm planting flowers in the dark
in hopes that they may bloom and bend
towards a source of light I can't yet see.
And when they do,
I'll know where to go,
not running from
but flying to.

Even if you can't see where you're going, even if you can't see the light, trust that it is there.

Sow the soil of your soul with seeds of joy, love and hope, and the flowers that bloom will find the light for you.

Dream, Girl

We squeeze our bodies and minds like lemons,
our lifeblood trickling out through clenched teeth,
the fragmented remains of our consciousness
seeping from the corners of glazed over eyes.
And it is only when we are wrung almost dry
that we are forced to stand up and fight our way
to the core of who we are,
plucking out our buried hearts
to crown our weary souls.

You owe it to yourself to live while you're alive. Crown yourself as your own hero and fight for your dreams. Fight for your life.

Sometimes, it's enough
to have gotten through the day
without having let go of your dreams.

Even if you have done nothing else, sometimes, it is enough to arrive at midnight still holding your dreams tight to your chest when, all through the day, they were being wrenched away from you.

Dream, Girl

I want to walk among mountains,
whet my heart on their jagged edges
and sky sharpened peaks,
forging a sense of being from nothing else but wonder.
One that will never again feel small,
even amid soaring mountain tops.
One that will understand the ancient language of the stars
that crown Her head
and always hear the moon song that calls to Her.

Whenever you start to feel small, let the earth remind you how to live—without limits, and without fear. Come back to the part of you that was birthed among mountains. The part of you that is still there, wild, free, and at home amidst snow-covered peaks drenched in moon glow and star light. Come back to the part of you that is larger than just this life alone. Let the greatest treasures of this earth remind you that you are as fierce and beautiful as the world around you.

Dream, Girl

Sometimes, it feels like we live one hundred lives within this one.
And at the end of each reincarnation,
when it feels like starting all over again,
know that we do not rise again from nothing,
but from the embers in the ashes.
We must gather the scattered fragments of our light, love, and lessons
and become again:
a new configuration
of Girl and Goddess.

We do not walk alone, that is sure. Every time you are pushed further into the ground or flung to the edge of what you thought you knew, when you are too tired to start over, know that you will rise again. And when you do, it will be on the shoulders of all those who have come before you and those who will come after. All the women, the goddesses, the witches, the rebels, and the revolutionaries; the women and girls who smiled and lived and learned in a world that didn't want them to. And don't forget all the versions of you—your past, present, and future—who will never stop reaching out their hands to pull you through the flames as you transform once more into a new configuration of the one you have always been and are always becoming.

You are not a star fallen,
for the stars themselves reside within you,
shining brightly in their wondrous masses—
a light that fills you up,
glittering beneath your skin.

Be not afraid of darkness, daughter of the moon, for you are made of stardust. Entire galaxies tumble through your veins—you are a world unto your own, with enough light in your heart, beneath your skin, and shining out from under heavy lids, to light up this world of yours many times over.

Dream, Girl

A butterfly flies out over the ocean
and I wonder if she too is looking for something else,
something that is so different from everything she has ever known—
a sense of freedom that will either drown her
or strengthen the steel in her wings.

Think about what you really want out of this one, exquisite lifetime. I hope you want more—not because you are lacking in anything, but because you are deserving of everything. Want more for yourself, from this life. Dream about those things. Then, dream bigger. Dream different. Dream without limit. And then, go after it all. You'll be surprised by the strength in your own wings.

The greatest rebellion
is the one you undertake against that in you that holds you back.
Face yourself.
Fight for your truth.
And already, you will be victorious.

Make rebellion a daily practice. Rebel against what you have been told, what you have been taught, and what you have been shown. Most of all, rebel against yourself. Rebel against that in you that says you are too much, or not enough. Rebel against that in you that says you can't make it or can't get what you want, what you deserve. Rebel against that in you that wants to step away from what lights you up, that wants to stop you from dreaming. Rebel again and again until you can distinguish what isn't true from what is really *you.*

Dreams are guiding stars
amidst the darkness of our unknown desires—
shimmering compasses
that point us in the direction
of our eternal purpose.

Pay attention to your outer world, the people and things around you and in front of you. But also pay attention to your inner world, your dreams, your daydreams, idle thoughts, and flights of fancy. For, when you see how your two worlds fit together, you will see the waiting path that has been carved for you beyond the horizon and among the stars.

Dream, Girl

She looked around with frank curiosity
laced with a kind of ferocity
that betrayed her outward desire
for a life as soft as summer nights.
Deep inside, She knew She was made for a life
that would tear through Her
as viciously as She clawed back in return,
until there was nothing left but shreds
of light and darkness and desire and wonder—
tatters in the wind
of a girl who lived life by her dreams.

We are brought up to ignore the shattered remains of generations of broken dreams underneath our feet; the constant barrage of knife-like words that scrape at our throats—sharp and ready to draw blood; the beasts that were taunted our whole lives—who now howl in the back of our minds.

And so, it takes a certain amount of ferocity to fight for a life that will be kind to you. A life that is soft in its acceptance and encouragement of your deepest desires.

Want the things you have been told you shouldn't have and can never possess. Wonder about the things you were told to ignore or accept without condition. And finally, dream without reason, logic or fear.

Finally, when your dreams get so big that your head and heart grow heavy, remember this well: you do not yield.

You do not yield
to the part of you that wants to give up, give in, and forgo
your innermost desires.
You do not yield
to those who would make you believe you are not worthy
of what you want.
You do not yield
to the voice inside and the many voices outside that would doubt
you.

Rally your heart and reinforce your mind to go to the ends of the
earth
for yourself.
Remember, you do not yield.

Acknowledgments

I would like to sincerely thank those in my life who have listened to my dreams, and encouraged me to keep dreaming.

About the Author

© Meghana Jayam

Julia Yee is a dreamer, reader, and writer who has called many corners of the world home. After a childhood spent in Saudi Arabia, she graduated from the University of St Andrews in Scotland and worked in finance in New York City for a few years before deciding to move to Paris to pursue her dreams and her writing more seriously. While forever dreaming, when she isn't wandering or reading, she posts original poetry on her Instagram page, writes YA fantasy, co-hosts Meet Me at the Bookstore, a literary podcast, and is pursuing a Master's in Creative Writing.

Connect with Julia on Instagram:
@day.dream.diaries

Learn more about the Meet Me at the Bookstore podcast:
@meetme_atthebookstore

About the Publisher

Indie Earth Publishing is an independent, author-first co-publishing company based in Miami, FL, dedicated to giving writers the creative freedom they deserve when publishing their poetry, fiction, and short story collections. Indie Earth provides its authors a plethora of services meant to aid them in their book publishing experiences and finally feel they are releasing the book of their dreams.

With Indie Earth Publishing, you are more than just an author, you are part of the Indie Earth creative family, making a difference one book at a time.

www.indieearthbooks.com

For inquiries, please email:
indieearthpublishinghouse@gmail.com

Instagram: @indieearthbooks

www.ingramcontent.com/pod-product-compliance
Ingram Content Group UK Ltd.
Pitfield, Milton Keynes, MK11 3LW, UK
UKHW021918270726
14059UKWH00002B/82